SFC

D0904695

CHORAL SINGING STEP BY STEP

JAMES JORDAN

SELECTED PUBLICATIONS BY JAMES JORDAN
AVAILABLE FROM GIA PUBLICATIONS, INC.

The Musician's Soul
(G-5095)

The Musician's Spirit
(G-5866)

The Musician's Walk
(G-6734)

Toward Center
The Art of Being for Musicians, Actors, Dancers, and Teachers
(G-7661)

The Musician's Breath
with Mark Moliterno and Nova Thomas
(G-7955)

Evoking Sound
Second Edition with DVD
(G-7359)

Dialogues II: The Inner Life of the Musician:
Coversations with Weston Noble
(CD-792)

The Anatomy of Conducting DVD
Architecture & Essentials: Choral and Instrumental
with Eugene Migliaro Corporon
(DVD-745)
Workbook (G-7358)

The Choral Rehearsal
Vol. 1: Techniques and Procedures (G-7128)
Vol. 2: Inward Bound–Philosophy and Score Preparation (G-7129)
The Choral Rehearsal DVD (DVD-720)

The Choral Warm-Up
(G-6397)
Accompanist Supplement, with accompaniment CD (G-6397A)
Modal Exercises, with accompaniment CD (G-6912)
Accompanied Canons for Choirs, with accompaniment CD (G-7145)
Index Card Pack (G-6397I)

Music for Conducting Study
with Giselle Wyers
(G-7359A)

CHORAL SINGING STEP BY STEP

ELEVEN CONCISE LESSONS FOR INDIVIDUAL OR CHORAL ENSEMBLE USE

JAMES JORDAN

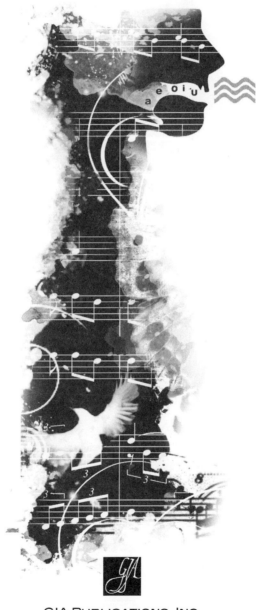

GIA PUBLICATIONS, INC.
CHICAGO

Choral Singing Step by Step
James Jordan

Art direction/design: Martha Chlipala

GIA Publications, Inc.
7404 S. Mason Ave
Chicago, IL 60638
www.giamusic.com

Copyright © 2011 GIA Publications, Inc.
All rights reserved.
Printed in the United States of America.

G-7934
ISBN: 978-1-57999-820-2

CONTENTS

PREFACE _____

Choral Singing Step by Step provides the basics of good singing technique. As I have often said to conductors, church musicians, music educators, and voice teachers, there are a few basic principles that can transform one's voice from a pedestrian sound into a beautiful tone. The major dilemma for most beginning or amateur singers (those who do not study voice regularly or have a degree in voice) is that they most often sing *on* their speaking voices—that is, they use the same sound or resonance as their speaking voice and sing using that voice. The principles presented in *Step by Step* show how to make the *transition* from speaking voice to singing voice and other basic important aspects of vocal technique.

Two of my teachers, Frauke Haasemann and Helen Kemp, always told me to give singers the *tools* of vocal technique—a collection of the basic techniques that allow a singer to produce a beautiful and free vocal sound. I have always believed that anyone can be taught to sing—and be taught to sing well. As with any skill, the mastery and understanding of the basics is essential not only to good singing, but also to the foundation of the many rewards that come from singing well.

The format of *Choral Singing Step by Step* is specifically designed for both individuals and groups. Following the instruction given here will greatly improve the sound you achieve when you sing. Use *Step by Step* as a beginning or as reinforcement in a journey already begun in either private or group study. Be sure to study the lessons in sequence, and to study them repeatedly. Read sections on your own, or use them at the beginning of rehearsal each week.

The principles in *Step by Step* know no age restriction. Good singing technique is good singing technique no matter the age or experience of the singer, and is applicable to those at every level of study. Regardless of the age or experience of a singer, revisiting the basics is an ongoing process. I teach and reinforce these principles regularly with my choirs at Westminster as well as church, community, and school choirs with which I work.

Mastery of these principles requires repeated review and practice. *Step by Step* not only provides basic instruction in vocal technique, but is also a resource for individuals, conductors, and choirs who wish to revisit and refresh these principles to ensure good, healthy, and free singing.

I hope this book helps you on your vocal journey.

—James Jordan

AN INTRODUCTION **FOR SINGERS**
_____ AND CONDUCTORS

For Singers

Conductors of ensembles at all levels as well as singers have often asked me, "Is there something I can do outside of rehearsal to improve my singing?" The answer, in short, is *Yes!*

The essentials of good singing are relatively simple concepts. But one must understand these concepts and then practice and reinforce them on a regular basis using some basic exercises. The exercises in *Choral Singing Step by Step,* while they may seem simple, are the route to the learning and constant reinforcement of these simple principles.

Both of my vocal technique mentors, Frauke Haasemann and Helen Kemp, always stressed that the essentials of singing are really quite simple...so simple that they remain elusive for many beginning singers. Simple exercises that teach easy-to-master skills form the foundation of singing technique. While *Step by Step* is certainly no substitute for private voice study, the principles presented here can greatly improve one's ability as a singer and contribute improved vocal ability to the choral ensemble's sound.

These exercises have been selected from a set of twenty-four that I wrote to form the vocal diet for any choral ensemble. The full set is found in the text *The Choral Warm-Up* (GIA Publications, G-6397) and separately as *The Choral Warm-Up: Core Vocal Exercises* (GIA Publications, G-6397A). Choral directors who use these exercises as a steady diet sing their praises. The eleven exercises chosen for *Step by Step* may seem basic, but through their use you will realize great strides in your singing.

For Conductors

Step by Step is designed to instill basic vocal know-how in your singers, and is also a vehicle by which they can practice at home. While many of us encourage our choirs to "learn their notes at home," the real issue is not the notes, but rather the vocal quality brought to the singing of those notes. An improvement in vocal tone has an immediate and dramatic effect on the pitch, intonation, and overall musicality of *any* ensemble.

All instrumental methods provide a book that instrumentalists take home and "practice out of." *Step by Step* serves the same purpose for choral singers. It is a small book that contains the essentials of vocal technique. Mastery of the simple principles in *Step by Step* will move every individual's singing forward.

Frauke Haasemann always said that singers need basic tools for their toolbox. *Step by Step* provides the necessary tools for your choral singers' toolbox. Learn these principles and revisit them regularly. Even a once-a-week review in your spare time will do much to improve not only your singing but also your confidence as a singer.

It is essential to place some degree of responsibility on singers for their voices. *Step by Step* gives your singers essential vocal information that will greatly improve your ensemble, and they can work on all of it outside of rehearsal. *As with instrumental music, this book should be in the possession of every singer in your choir.* This is not a manual for conductors to use in rehearsal; it is a book for individual use. Reinforce the principles set out in its pages in your warm-up procedures.

The material presented here parallels the material in *The Choral Warm-Up*. Using that book together with *Step by Step* provides the strongest vocal/pedagogical framework for both individual beginning vocal study and the planning and execution of the choral warm-up in rehearsal.

Learning to hear vocal problems in choirs is always challenging for the conductor. *The Choral Conductor's Aural Tutor* (GIA, G-6905) will help you hear and diagnose vocal issues within your choir. Adding it to *Step by Step* and *The Choral Warm-Up* can take your choir a long way toward the goal of beautiful choral singing.

HOW TO USE STEP BY STEP_____

Exercise Melodies

Starting on page 18 are six exercises chosen for daily practice. They precede the eleven lessons for improving singing that make up the body of *Step by Step* because they will form the basis of your vocal practice. Learn these melodies well.

The recorded examples provided (available at www.giamusic.com/stepbystep) proceed by half steps and end after appropriate repetition. The exercises can be performed with or without accompaniment; however, I encourage you to use the accompaniments provided because this reinforces good intonation. Use the vowel sounds suggested for each exercise.

Working through the Lessons

After learning the melodies of these exercises, work through each lesson of *Step by Step* in sequence and apply the vocal principle presented to one or more of the exercises below. Make these exercises the subject of your individual practice sessions.

It may be helpful to record your singing so that you can hear your own voice and begin to self-monitor your sound. Remember that what you want to achieve is a consistent sound throughout each exercise. Don't forget to apply the suggested physical gestures as you sing the exercises. When you hear or sense a good sound, always remember what that good sound felt like.

A Final Reminder

Do not practice with headphones. Practice only with the recording with an audio playback. Singing with headphones prevents you from singing in tune with something other than yourself. Singing is not an act of hearing yourself, but rather listening to everything *but* yourself. Wearing headphones while singing can create severe vocal problems. Always practice with the exercises being played through an external sound source.

Enjoy your practice!

EXERCISE MELODIES _____

Here are your six exercise melodies. They will form the core of your practice. Sigh downward on *oo* between exercises. Sighing is the best vocal therapy there is to keep your voice in healthy singing shape.

> MP3 versions of accompaniments for these melodies are available at www.giamusic.com/stepbystep.

General Instructions

Suggested Syllables

Sing on the syllables *noo* or *nee,* or substitute *du* or *dee* if you like.

- Syllables beginning with the consonant *d* can allow you to use your breath more efficiently.

- Be aware of the position of your tongue for each of the vowels you sing as explained below.

Singing oo

- Make the tongue flat in the mouth and imagine a small pit or indentation in the tongue.

- Round the lips as though wrapping them around the sound.

Singing ee

- Arch the tongue high in the mouth and rest the tip on the lower front teeth.

- Find the correct position by saying the word *see* and bringing awareness to the tongue's place in the mouth.

Consonant d

- When singing on the consonant *d*, make certain that your tongue is pointed and touching the ridge above your upper gum line.

MELODY 1.

Starting key of recorded exercise:

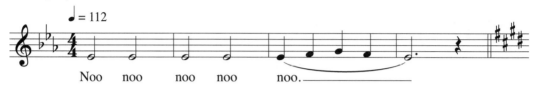

Noo   noo   noo   noo   noo.———

Ending key of recorded exercise:

Noo   noo   noo   noo   noo.———

MELODY 2.

Starting key of recorded exercise:

Nee   voo   nee   voo   nee   voo   nee   voo

nee voo nee voo nee voo nee voo nee.

Ending key of recorded exercise:

Nee   voo   nee   voo   nee   voo   nee   voo

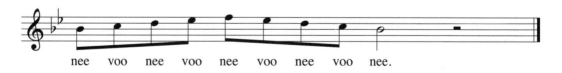

nee voo nee voo nee voo nee voo nee.

MELODY 3.

Starting key of recorded exercise:

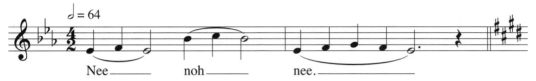

Nee⸺ noh⸺ nee.⸺

Ending key of recorded exercise:

Nee⸺ noh⸺ nee.⸺

MELODY 4.

Starting key of recorded exercise:

Dee dee dee dee dee   dee dee dee dee dee   doh.⸺

Ending key of recorded exercise:

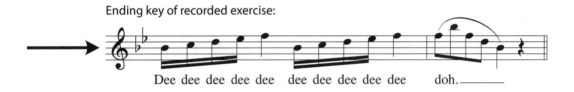

Dee dee dee dee dee   dee dee dee dee dee   doh.⸺

MELODY 5.

Starting key of recorded exercise:

Nee voo nee voo nee voo nee voo   nee voo nee voo nee.
Nee————— noo—————   nee— noo— nee.

Ending key of recorded exercise:

Nee voo nee voo nee voo nee voo   nee voo nee voo nee.
Nee————— noo—————   nee— noo— nee.

MELODY 6.

Starting key of recorded exercise:

Dee dee dee   dee dee dee   doh————— dee dee dee.

Ending key of recorded exercise:

Dee dee dee   dee dee dee   doh————— dee dee dee.

ALIGNMENT AND LENGTHENING_____

Alignment and Body Awareness

The singer uses his body both to sustain life and to cultivate his art. He can never escape from himself, for his physical life either furthers or hinders his artistic life. A good singing teacher and choir director will utilize activities from everyday life as well as natural and acquired capabilities of the body for development of his artistic work. On the other hand, the experiences and demands of the artistic life will influence the everyday life of the singers. (p. 2)

—Wilhelm Ehmann
Choral Directing

The purpose of Body Mapping is to provide a context for vocal technique rather than the technique itself. Vocal technique varies greatly across styles of choral singing, but context for each style is the same. Body awareness, an adequate and accurate Body Map, and freedom from tension serve the members of a jazz choir as well as they will serve a cathedral choir or a gospel choir, though the members are singing with different techniques. (p. 13)

Profound embodiment is also the key to ensemble. Singers' continuous, intimate, often intense awareness of their own bodies (sensations, movements, and emotions) is the ideal condition for feeling and responding to each other and to the conductor. Then a chorus is a chorus and not just a collection of individuals singing at the same time. The many choral conductors who have helped their singers regain full body awareness as they sing are surprised and delighted by the terrific difference embodiment makes in the quality of the singing. (p. 14)

—Barbara Conable
*The Structures and Movement
of Breathing*

Learning Alignment Awareness: Employ Body Mapping Principles to Re-Educate Your Body

Body Mapping is a principle that has been championed by Barbara Conable in her application of the principles of Alexander Technique. In my opinion, the most important aspect of learning to sing as an *ensemble* is Body Mapping and the understanding of its principles. An understanding of Body Mapping allows for an unlocking of all other aspects of vocal technique. In fact, depending on the singer, this information alone can create a body that will sing better, thus enabling the choir to sing well without this information as a group. Your Body Map is how you actually process your body and use it in singing. With a wrong map, it is impossible to sing well.

Alignment vs. Posture

Many of us were taught either by design or experience that the cue word for all things concerning the body usage is *posture* (the P word!). Singers should abandon the use of that word in their vocabulary for a simple reason: it recalls every image of body alignment we have acquired throughout our lives—most, if not all, of which are incorrect for singing. A primary role of vocal study is to provide a new mental paradigm that forms the foundation for healthy vocalism. The better word for this newly taught and discovered body awareness is *alignment*. Align thyself!

Read the following quote to gain an understanding of the importance of your Body Map.

Our Body Maps are our physical self-representations. We literally map our own bodies with our brains, that is, we conceive neurally what we're like (structure), what we do (function), and how big we are (size). We map our whole bodies in this regard, and we map their parts. If our Body Maps are accurate, we move well. If our Body Maps are inconsistent with the reality of our structures, we do not move well. Singing is movement, and its quality is as determined by our Body Maps as the quality of our walking is. Fortunately, inaccurate or inadequate Body Maps can be replaced with accurate and adequate Body Maps. All that is needed is information and attention to information. Human beings are naturally self-correcting, and our Body Maps are no exception. (p. 13)

—Barbara Conable
The Structures and Movement
of Breathing

What Is a Body Map?

The study of the science of somatics provides us with compelling information concerning the power of the brain in determining the use and misuse of the body for many of life's activities, including singing and the singing process. Simply stated, somatics tells us that our Body Maps determine how we perceive, and therefore how we use, our bodies. The Body Map is the acquired mental picture of the function and structure of the body. This is a powerful statement that has profound and far-reaching implications for how we teach choirs and how they learn, with consequent implications for the choral rehearsal.

Body Mapping can best be described using the old adage that a picture is worth a thousand words. Body Mapping includes mental maps for *body size, structure,* and *correct usage.* If the Body Map is incorrect, incorrect body usage is the result. However, once a Body Map is corrected and reinforced, it remains corrected forever—a simple and powerful concept that, until recently, has been ignored in the way we conduct our choral rehearsals. Incorporation of this principle profoundly changes the depth of the warm-up process and the entire direction of vocal study.

Learning the Core of the Body:
The Six Points of Alignment

After the activities that deconstruct our daily poor postural habits, we must spend a portion of each practice session reconstructing alignment. Initially, this must include learning that provides for new Body Maps. In later stages of your warm-up's evolution, you must then only reinforce and call into awareness your new Body Map. As Barbara Conable so beautifully puts it, you must use your practice to give yourself a "piece of the truth"—the truth about body alignment.

This part of your instruction includes learning the six points of alignment. For more detailed instruction, watch the DVD *Move Well, Avoid Injury* (GIA, DVD-839). Once you understand these principles, incorporate them into your daily practice. Begin by studying the following diagram. Imagine your body is organized like an apple is organized around it's core.

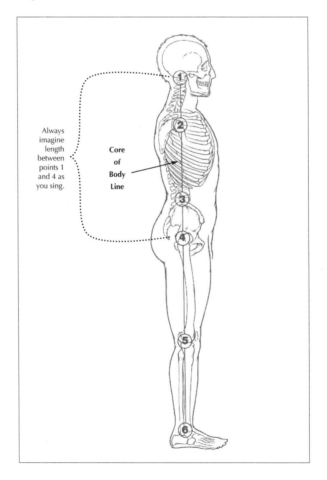

FIGURE 1.1. SIX POINTS OF ALIGNMENT.

Six Points of Skeletal Balance

Correct Map of the Hips

The balance of the upper half of the body over the legs. (see ④ in Figure 1.1).

Correct Map of the A/O Joint

The balance of the head on the spine at the center–You should be able to gently nod your head "yes" when the A/O joint is balanced and free.

Correct Map of the Pelvis: The Core of the Body

The balance of the thorax on the massive lumbar vertebrae at the center–The pelvis is located within the hips.

Correct Map of the Shoulders

The balance of the arm structures over the spine at the center.

Correct Map of the Knees

The balance of the knees, loose but not locked.

Correct Map of the Feet

The balance of the body on the arches of the feet at the center.

What is the *feeling* of being aligned? After reviewing the points of balance:

1. Lean forward. Ask yourself: Do I feel tension in my lower back?

2. Come to center, moving your body to a place where you feel that *no work is being done*. Always imagine length between points one and four on the diagram as you sing.

3. Now lean backward. Do you feel tightness or tension?

4. Return to center where *no work is being done*.

When alignment is correct, the body is in balance. You will always feel as though *no work is being done*. That feeling is the goal of an accurate map of skeletal balance or core points of balance of the body.

As shown in *Move Well, Avoid Injury* (GIA, DVD-839), place a star or notebook reinforcement on each point of balance as you learn about it. This activity, although simple, ensures that the Body Map is correctly acquired. These essential points of balance are presented below. The order is different from the DVD. It moves from the most inaccurately perceived and important points of balance to the lesser ones, but all must be properly mapped for alignment to be correct and for a total body awareness to take over.

Using Verbal Reminders to Reinforce Awareness

Constant verbal reminders concerning your awareness are of central importance to your singing. In a private voice lesson, the voice teacher assumes the role of alignment monitor. As soon as a student becomes misaligned or unaware, the teacher perceives it and gives the appropriate correction. However, due to the group dynamic of the choral rehearsal, singers may lose touch with their bodies— that is, become perceptually unaware of their bodies, without correction. They become perceptually numb. To overcome this, simply ask yourself, "Am I aware of my entire body as I sing?"

The Proper Use of Rehearsal Room Chairs

Most chairs in choral rehearsal rooms, unfortunately, are not designed to encourage good alignment. However, with a simple technique, most chairs can be rendered useable.

1. When you sing, place one leg back and under the chair. This will ensure a more correct alignment of the core of the body, specifically, the pelvis.

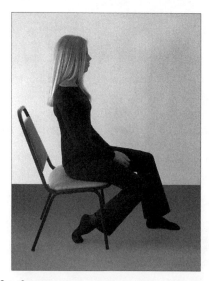

FIGURE 1.2. CORRECT USE OF A REHEARSAL ROOM CHAIR.

2. Make certain chairs are of the correct height. Many of the chairs in choral rehearsal rooms are stackable. It is important, if possible, to adjust chair height by stacking chairs according to the height of the singer. Most chairs are designed for singers of average height (5'6" to 5'10"). For shorter singers, a box or hymnals may be used to avoid dangling legs that do not contact the floor. For taller singers, chairs can be stacked accordingly. The rule of thumb is that the thigh and shinbone should form a 90-degree angle when height is correct.

FIGURE 1.3. STACKING CHAIRS TO ACHIEVE PROPER CHAIR HEIGHT.

The Use of Music and Folders in Rehearsal

There is a great deal of alignment sabotage that occurs in a choral rehearsal when choral octavos or choir folders are used. After remapping the core of the body, the use of music may destroy your work. When you look at your music, you usually drag your neck forward, and this destroys the independence and mobility that correct alignment fosters in the A/O joint. To avoid this, simply *tilt your head to see the music.*

Self-Verbal Alignment Cues for Singing Alignment

Ask yourself these questions while you practice and are in group rehearsal:

- Are you singing with your whole body?

- Are you keeping your head independent and mobile?

- Are you thinking up, over, and up?

- How is the joint of your head to your spine? Is it free? Can you sense it?

- Are you remembering your weight-bearing spine, at your core?

- Are you balanced at your hip joints?

- Are your knees released and flexible?

- Are your feet feeling the floor?

- Are you feeling the tripod of your feet's arches?

- Is your head dynamically poised?

- Is your back free? long and wide?

- Are you organized around your spine, like an apple around a core?

- When you look at your music, are you tilting your head? Don't drag your head forward.

- Are you balancing your arms? Don't pull them back or slump down.

Video deomonstrations of all of the physical gestures in this book can be viewed at
www.giamusic.com/stepbystep.

LESSON TWO

THE SIGH: LEARNING THE "CAVE"_____

Spaciousness and Proper Vocal Production through the Use of the Sigh: Relaxation of the Vocal Tract—Creating Space

I prefer tone quality to be varied. I must say that tone quality is more consistent among the great voices than among untrained and amateur voices. One of the problems in training voices is that since the world rewards singers on the size of the voice as well as on its beauty, or perhaps more on size than beauty, a lot of voices are forced beyond their physical capacity. Not everybody can be an Olympic Champion weightlifter. But most vocal studios, it seems to me, put their emphasis on developing a voice of size rather than on developing a voice of pitch integrity or quality. (p. 68)

—Robert Shaw
In Quest of Answers

Singing is like yawning. Many have misunderstood and tried to do both at the same time, hoping thereby to super induce the feeling of an "open throat." (p. 111)

—Giovanni Battista Lamperti
Vocal Wisdom

The use of the sigh is one of the most valuable tools available to singers to determine the overall health of the vocal mechanism. Don't underestimate its power as a diagnostic tool. A complete understanding of the proper technical execution of the sigh is at the core of all vocal instruction. Stated another way, if you cannot execute the sigh in a vocally correct way, then *all* consequent vocalism will suffer. The recipe for the correct performance of a vocal sigh is as follows:

Learning the Downward Sigh

1. Always sigh *downward* on *oo*. Make sure you imagine a pit in your tongue and your lips are wrapped around the sound.

2. Create space through the use of the cave.

3. Keep the soft palate slightly raised throughout the sigh.

4. Make sure the vocal sound remains *high* and *forward* as the sound descends in pitch. Put the heel of your hand on your forehead to help keep the sound high and forward.

5. Focus on wrapping your lips around the sound.

6. Use reinforcing physical gestures to ensure these points are successfully accomplished. Always use the up, over, and up gesture as you sigh. (See the section on this gesture below.)

Important: Begin your sigh in an "apartment" that is above your nose in the top of your head. Keep your sound in that "apartment" as you sigh downward.

I. Always sigh downward on oo.

The sounds *oo* and *ee* contain the most amount of head tone of all the vowels in all voices, but especially in women's and treble voices. To produce a good *oo* vowel, make certain the tongue is in a flat position in the mouth and imagine that the tongue has a pit in it. Also make sure the lips are rounded and are truly participating in the production of the vowel. Imagining this shape tends to counterbalance any tongue tension you may bring to the vocalism from speech.

2. Create space through the use of the cave.

Many vocal problems of amateur singers are the result of their inability to create a proper spaciousness within the oral cavity. This ability is a central component to good vocal technique; in fact, it is the principal building block of healthy vocal production.

The steps for learning the *cave* are as follows:

a. Feel for the fleshy cartilage at the front of the ear hole. Place a finger just forward of that point.

b. Once you locate that point, slowly drop your jaw until you feel an indentation or a cave.

c. Create a small cave rather than a large one. A larger cave indicates hyperextension of the jaw.

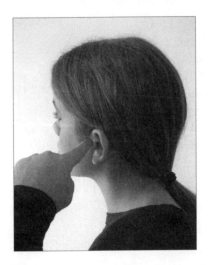

FIGURE 2.1. LOCATING THE CAVE.

FIGURE 2.2. DROPPING THE JAW USING THE CAVE.

3. Make certain the soft palate remains slightly raised throughout the sigh.

Most inexperienced singers sing with a soft palate that is too low to direct vocal resonances into the masque (the resonant bone structures in the face). The proper position is analogous to the position of the soft palate approximately one-quarter to one-half of the way through a yawn. Once in that position, the palate should remain in that raised position throughout the singing.

Maintaining a raised palate throughout the singing process performs another very important technical aspect in the voice-building process: keeping the soft palate raised avoids register breaks and a mixing of vocal registers can be accomplished in a natural, healthy fashion.

4. Make sure the vocal sound remains high and forward as the sound descends in pitch.

Another serious problem for inexperienced singers, especially singers whose native tongue is American English, is that sounds tend to be produced too far back in the mouth. Hence, vocal sounds are dull and unresonant, which results in poor pitch (a flatness and dullness in the sound). So you must constantly reinforce the correct feeling of high and forward sound. The use of physical gesture is the most efficient way to accomplish this.

a. As you sigh downward on *oo*, place the heel of your hand on your forehead (Figure 2.3). This gesture naturally ensures that the sound is high and forward.

b. Perform the sigh without your hand on your forehead.

c. Now perform the sigh with your hand on your forehead again.

d. With your hand on your forehead, you will hear a more brilliant and resonant sound.

FIGURE 2.3. USE OF THE HAND TO REINFORCE HIGH AND
FORWARD SOUND PLACEMENT.

5. Focus on wrapping your lips around the sound.

American English that is further influenced by regional dialects produces vowel sounds that tend to be resonantly spread and dull in sound. To counter this default tendency, *wrap your lips around the sound*. This accomplishes two important objectives. First, wrapping your lips around the sound maintains internal vertical spaciousness. Remember that this space is created by finding the cave and must be maintained. Second, you begin to learn vowel modification—that is, the ability to influence both the focus of the pitch and the color of the vowel. It is important, however, to have the correct Body Map to know exactly what rounding is in this process. It is not "lipstick lips" that create this, but rather the muscles that surround the mouth.

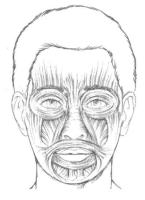

FIGURE 2.4. CORRECT BODY MAP OF THE LIPS.

Video deomonstrations of all of the physical gestures in this book can be viewed at
www.giamusic.com/stepbystep.

6. Use reinforcing physical gestures to ensure these points are successfully accomplished.

One of the challenges in learning to sing is certainly discovering how to maintain a type of vocal/technical accountability and consistency. In the private voice studio, this is easier to monitor and achieve because of the one-on-one nature of the instruction. But when practicing alone, two problems are rampant. First, too much technique tends to get lost in unawareness until it is made habitual. Second, it is difficult to self-monitor and know that you are doing all of the technical things learned.

The way to accomplish personal vocal/technical accountability is through the use of physical gestures as a type of constant reinforcement until the correct singing sensations and awarenesses take over. Throughout this guide, physical gestures are suggested for reinforcing many of the vocal principles you will learn. Using these gestures can bring a vibrant vocal accountability into both individual singing and ensemble rehearsal that ensures correct vocal technique results. Do not underestimate either their power or their potency.

Use the Up, Over, and Up Gesture to Reinforce the Sigh

The gesture for reinforcing all aspects of the sigh is called the up, over, and up gesture, which is shown in Figures 2.5 through 2.7. *Always* use the gesture suggested here when you perform the sigh after learning about its various components. End the exercise at the bottom of your sigh with a hand on your forehead as shown above in Figure 2.3.

FIGURE 2.5. BEGINNING POSITION FOR THE UP, OVER,
AND UP SIGH GESTURE: *START*.

FIGURE 2.6. SECOND HAND POSITION IN THE UP, OVER,
AND UP SIGH GESTURE SEQUENCE: *OVER*.

FIGURE 2.7. THIRD HAND POSITION IN THE UP, OVER, AND UP SIGH GESTURE SEQUENCE: *CONCLUDING UP.* ALTERNATIVELY, THIS GESTURE MAY BE ENDED WITH THE HEEL OF THE HAND ON THE FOREHEAD AS GIVEN IN FIGURE 2.4.

What You Should Hear When the Sigh Is Technically Correct

The quality of the downward sigh should be *light* and *airy*. Remember that the primary objective of the sigh is to create space and to lower the vocal mechanism to a place where it can optimally function. This sound, which should be high and forward, manifests itself to the ear as brilliant, colorful, and vibrant. The idea is to avoid a dull, flat pitch. Focus the vowel by rounding the lips (wrapping the lips around the sound) to produce a sound that is narrow, not spread. If the idea of a high and forward sound is confusing, simply sigh with the heel of your hand on your forehead. This gesture produces a high and forward sound.

Note that what you hear is an important aspect of not only this particular exercise, but of each of the techniques presented in *Step by Step.* Your ability to diagnose *and* correct is directly related to what you can hear, and more importantly, *feel.* This discriminating listening and self-awareness is an important part of the learning process.

INHALATION AND EXHALATION _____

The Breath: The Core of Rehearsal Technique

Therefore, the basic trick is in the preparatory upbeat. It is exactly like breathing: the preparation is like an inhalation, and the music sounds like an exhalation. We all have to inhale in order to speak, for example; all verbal expression is exhaled. So it is with music: we inhale on the upbeat and sing out a phrase of music, then inhale again and breathe out the next phrase. A conductor who breathes with the music has gone far in acquiring a technique. (p. 272)

—Leonard Bernstein
in *The Conductor's Art*

As a singer, one of the most influential tools in your singing arsenal is the breath. Breathing directly influences tempo, tone color, shape of phrase, ensemble dynamic, and spiritual content of the tone. *There* never *should be a "hold" or "locking" between inhalation and singing.*

Understanding Inhalation and Exhalation

In my experience, the major factor impeding proper inhalation and exhalation in singers is a misconception as to how the breath works in an anatomical sense. One of the most valuable rehearsal techniques for understanding this breathing process is called *eight-handed breathing.*

Central to an understanding of the breath process is knowing what happens anatomically when breath enters into the body. What part of the body moves first, second, third, and fourth? If you do not understand this process, then your tone quality is adversely affected.

Memorize this phrase: *Air comes into my body like a wave from top to bottom.*

The Body Mechanics of Breathing

When inhalation occurs, the following parts of the body move in *this* order (Figure 3.1):

1. *Ribs of the back*
   Traverse or travel outward, each rib traveling at its own rate.

2. *Diaphragm*
   Moves from a more-domed to a less-domed position.

3. *Abdominal walls*
   Both front and sides move outward.

4. *Pelvic floor*
   Drops slightly.

Using the hands as a physical representation of the inhalation process, the sequence looks like this:

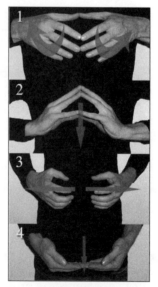

FIGURE 3.1. INHALATION.

Remember that these things happen in sequence: one, two, three, and four. *Air comes into my body like a wave from top to bottom.* Note that inhalation *always* occurs in this order, with all of these body parts always participating.

When exhalation occurs, the following parts of the body move in this order (Figure 3.2):

1. *Ribs of the back*
   Traverse or travel inward, each rib traveling at its own rate.

2. *Diaphragm*
   Moves from a less-domed to a more-domed position.

3. *Abdominal walls*
   Both front and sides move inward.

4. *Pelvic floor*
   Raises slightly.

The order for exhalation is the same as inhalation: one, two, three, and four, not four, three, two, one. Using the hands as a physical representation of the exhalation process, the sequence looks like this:

FIGURE 3.2. EXHALATION.

It is important to understand that the order of movement of the anatomy of the body is the same for exhalation as it is for inhalation. Many singers believe that, anatomically, the exhalation process is the reverse of the inhalation process, but this is a perceptual fantasy. Correction of this misnomer will dramatically improve tone and expressivity.

It bears repeating that inhalation and exhalation happen in a sequence from top to bottom. Say this phrase with every breath:

Air comes into my body like a wave from top to bottom.

LESSON FOUR

SINGING ON THE BREATH ———————

Breathing: Learning Support, or On-the-Breath Singing

Once you have remapped the inhalation and exhalation process using the eight-handed breathing method, you are ready to learn what is called *support*. A synonym for this is the phrase *singing on the breath*. Technically, this is the process by which breath, movement of air, and phonation are all interconnected in one bodily sensation to produce a vibrant, beautiful tone. This is the goal: to experience these interconnected activities as a single bodily sensation rather than as separate component parts.

In my experience, it is most efficient to experience support after remapping the inhalation and exhalation process. Support is a complex interaction of breath and phonation that can be difficult for the novice singer to understand. It is most efficiently learned through a singular exercise that is both quick and efficient. Some describe this as the *breath kneading exercise*.

Learning the Breath Kneading Exercise

1. Select a simple exercise melody from the front of this book, preferably one with upward leaps, such as melody 3 or 5.

2. Put your left hand in an open, flat position at navel level. This subconsciously locates the depth necessary for a supported breath (Figure 4.1).

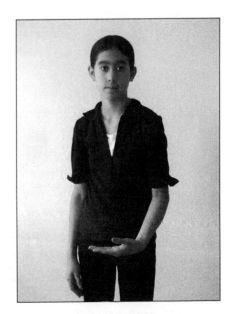

FIGURE 4.1. LEFT-HAND POSITION IN THE BREATH KNEADING EXERCISE.

3. Now move the right hand in a circular forward motion (Figure 4.2). Note that the hand should be held in a fist, with thumb facing forward. The fist *gently* contacts the left hand at the bottom of the circle. Also make note of the size of the circle made by the right hand. The speed of the right hand should be the tempo of the exercise or composition you are practicing. Note that the movement of the right hand also represents physically the constant movement of air in the singing process.

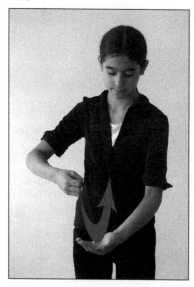

FIGURE 4.2. RIGHT-HAND MOVEMENT IN THE BREATH KNEADING EXERCISE.

FIGURE 4.3.
RIGHT-HAND SEQUENTIAL CIRCULAR MOVEMENT IN THE BREATH KNEADING
EXERCISE, FRONT VIEW.

FIGURE 4.4.
RIGHT-HAND SEQUENTIAL CIRCULAR MOVEMENT IN THE BREATH KNEADING
EXERCISE, RIGHT SIDE VIEW.

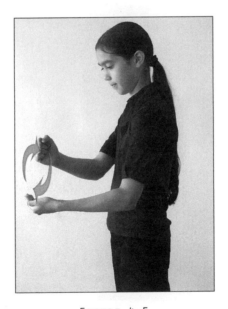

FIGURE 4.5.
RIGHT-HAND SEQUENTIAL CIRCULAR MOVEMENT IN THE BREATH KNEADING
EXERCISE, LEFT SIDE VIEW.

4. After you learn the motions for breath kneading, connect them
    to the exercise melodies suggested above (3 or 5). Remember: *Air
    comes into my body like a wave from top to bottom.* Perform the
    exercises in sequence, moving up a half step each time, with a breath
    between each repetition. Be certain the circular motion of the right
    hand never stops or slows throughout your singing. The sensation
    you feel while performing this exercise is support, or on-the-breath
    singing. It is important for you to label this sensation.

5. After you have sung the exercise melody correctly with the breath
    kneading motions detailed above, it is important to experience off-
    the-breath singing. Learning occurs when you are able to distinguish
    when one thing is not another. To do this, simply raise your hands
    to upper-chest or neck level and sing the exercise again (Figure 4.6).
    Immediately label the very different sound you produce and feel as
    an off-the-breath sound, which is undesirable in singing.

FIGURE 4.6. RIGHT-HAND HIGH SEQUENTIAL CIRCULAR MOVEMENT IN THE
BREATH KNEADING EXERCISE, ILLUSTRATING THE SENSATION OF INCORRECT OR
OFF-THE-BREATH SINGING.

CREATING SOUND TO SING "ON": TRANSITIONING FROM YOUR SPEAKING VOICE TO YOUR SINGING VOICE _____

Building Resonance

> Each singer has a different physiognomy and, therefore, a slightly different sense of focus. This precludes a teacher being able to direct a tone to a specific place such as "behind the front teeth," "in the nose," and "in the sinuses." As a student achieves a certain amount of vocal freedom and coordination of the various parts of the vocal mechanism, as well as a good mental concept of the sound he should be making, proper focus will result. (p. 96)

> —Richard Miller
> *The Structure of Singing*

Creating General Resonances

Of all the steps in the voice-building process, this is the one that is either most often missed or performed at the wrong point in the vocal study sequence. If this step is not taught and achieved at the appropriate point in the learning process, then the vocalism for the rest of the practice session becomes unruly and, at times, unuseable. If this step is omitted, irreversible vocal damage is created for the rest of that particular practice period.

Also note that if this step is omitted, you will likely begin singing with the resonances you have used in your speaking voice all day. Not only are those resonances insufficient sound "fuel" for the singing process, but it is also necessary to move through a resonantial transition between speaking and singing.

Correct and healthy singing resonances and the physical "homes" or "apartments" of those resonances must be awakened and activated. The most efficient route to those resonances is through humming and chewing exercises.

Remember that the purpose of these exercises, in addition to the sigh, is to transition your voice from speaking to singing.

Here are the techniques for learning these exercises:

Humming and Chewing: Resonance-Generating Exercises

1. Hum and chew in your middle register on the consonant *m,* as in *mmmm.*

2. Keep the teeth apart and lips lightly together.

3. Make certain the hum and chew is spacious. Check your cave (Figures 2.1 and 2.2).

4. Keep the sound high and forward. To ensure this and prevent the sound from resting in the jowels, *place the heel of your hand on your forehead* as you hum and chew.

5. To make certain resonances are generated in all registers of the voice, hum and chew also in the upper and lower registers.

6. To ensure there is enough head tone in the sound, it is often helpful to immediately follow each humming and chewing exercise with a downward sigh on *oo* and the appropriate supporting hand gesture.

Specific Resonances:
Developing a "Sleeve" for your Sound (*mm, nn*)

After you have created a general resonance through humming and chewing voiced consonants, it is then the task of your vocal study to further refine that resonance into an appropriate sound. Is the sound you need bright or dark? This is dependent upon the music to be sung. I have found that the terms *bright* and *dark* are somewhat dangerous to employ because of the inconsistency of the meaning of those words when translated in each individual singer's mind. How bright or how dark should a sound be? It is all relative to one's perception. Overly bright sounds may translate into sounds produced with a high larynx or excessively high palate.

Sounds that are too dark may be the result of a jowel placement that is too far back, or from a tension-ridden tongue. Both extremes must be avoided.

Here are two approaches that are effective in further focusing general resonances. One approach is to imagine either a *tall and narrow* vowel or a *round* vowel. In the warm-up you *must* make a choice. If you do not, you will usually default to the vowel shape most closely associated with your speaking dialect. Simply visualizing the shape of the vowel will generate the appropriate resonances. Also, by using this approach, you have begun to build diction through appropriate vowel color.

The second approach is to affect vowel color through breath. For a brighter vowel color, take a *cool* breath. For a darker vowel color, take a *warm* breath. For the darker vowel colors, it may be helpful to once again place the heel of your hand on your forehead to ensure high and forward placement.

Developing Specific Resonances

Make a choice:

1. Sing vowels that are either tall and narrow or round.

    —or—

2. Take either a *cool* breath to encourage brighter resonances or a *warm* breath to favor darker resonances.

Then:

3. Begin your practice on the vowels *oo* and *ee* only.

4. Sometimes it is helpful to sing exercises on the word *ming* with a somewhat strident tone (See page 55). Because we tend to sing with our speaking voices, some singers must vocalize with a strident, almost ugly sound to bring the voice high and forward. After achieving a high and forward placement of the voice, immediately do an exercise in a normal singing tone.

THE HELPER VOWELS: *OO* AND *EE*_____

Interdependent Relationship and Pedagogy of the oo and ee Vowels

The *oo* and *ee* vowels are the most important vowels for building a healthy vocal sound. Once you are familiar with these vowels and can clearly sing them, then it is necessary to further define the vowel color. Without correction, the *oo* vowel generally lacks color and pitch core because it is sung too far back in the mouth "jowel vowel" and does not utilize the maximum resonant space. The *ee* vowel is generally too open and is overly bright because of a lack of vertical spaciousness. Hence, to build healthy *oo* and *ee* vowels, the *oo* vowel must contain elements of *ee* and the *ee* vowel must contain elements of *oo*. To achieve this, do the following:

1. For the *oo* vowel, *imagine* an *ee* vowel behind it. This will infuse the *oo* sound with a bit more brightness that will clarify the vowel's pitch core.

2. For the *ee* vowel, wrap your lips around the sound and *imagine* an *oo* vowel behind the sung *ee*. This will infuse the *ee* sound with a bit more of the quality of an *oo* vowel. A rounder, more spacious *ee* vowel will be the result.

Practice these concepts using one or more exercise melodies. Learn what good sound is by discovering what it isn't. **Practice making poor oo and ee vowels, followed by the correct versions of these sounds.**

BUILDING CORE SOUND _____

The sound of your voice is determined primarily by two acoustic factors:

1. How much space is in the sound as created by the sigh taught in Lesson Two, and

2. How that sound is balanced by an equal amount of sound generated by the bones in your face, usually called the *masque*.

Balancing these two areas of your voice not only creates a beautiful sound, but also produces an acoustic condition that allows your sound to be in tune.

Many of us who have had little vocal training sing with the voice we speak with. For Americans, that sound usually sits far back in the mouth, producing what I call a "jowel vowel." In order to sing with a beautiful sound that can hold pitch accurately, we must learn to "bring the sound high and forward," that is, to a place different than where we speak.

For beautiful tone, we must use both parts of our sound arsenal: space created by the sigh (i.e., the cave) mixed with high and forward resonances. When we produce these resonances correctly, they feel as if they are sitting in the cheekbones or directed toward the front teeth. There are several simple exercises you can learn to gain access to this valuable part of your sound.

As you experiment with these techniques, make sure that you are breathing well and feeling the breath in your body as when you did the breath kneading exercise in Lesson Four.

Using Physical Gestures

Perhaps the easiest and most efficient way to acquire a "high and forward" sound is to simply use one of the following gestures while singing one of the exercise melodies. Note that each gesture creates a decidedly different sound. Repeated practice with these simple physical movements develops a type of vocal muscle memory that can recall the correct sound. The cue for you as a singer is how that sound *felt* as you produced it. Once experienced, all of these different sounds are available for your use when singing.

Video deomonstrations of all of the physical gestures in this book can be viewed at www.giamusic.com/stepbystep.

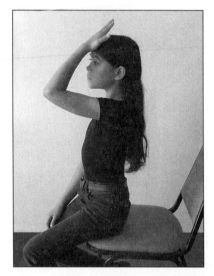

FIGURE 7.1. HEEL OF HAND ON FOREHEAD.

This is the *most* efficient physical exercise to bring your sound immediately to a "high and forward" place.

FIGURE 7.2. HIGH AND FORWARD FINGER WAND (THE *OO* MAGNET).

FIGURE 7.3. CONGEALING SOUND MIXING GESTURE: BEGINNING POSITION.

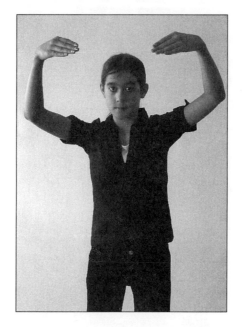

FIGURE 7.4. CONGEALING SOUND MIXING GESTURE: MIDDLE POSITION.

FIGURE 7.5. CONGEALING SOUND MIXING GESTURE: END POSITION.

FIGURE 7.6. CONGEALING SOUND MIXING GESTURE:
UNDESIRABLE END POSITION.

Exercises to Create Forward Resonance and Move from the Speaking Voice to the Singing Voice

Bad Smell

Sing one of the exercise melodies as if you smell a horrible odor. Wrinkle your nose a bit. After singing this way several times, return to your "regular" singing voice. You will notice a difference in your sound.

Widen Your Molars

Sing one of the exercise melodies while imagining that your back molars are spreading apart.

Ming/Yeh

This is singing on the nasty part of your voice. Sometimes it is helpful as a part of your daily practice to sing with an ugly sound. By doing this you can access the "high and forward" resonances that color your voice. Choose an exercise melody or sing the descending five-note scale in Figure 7.7 on a nasal, almost ugly sound at a *forte* dynamic level on the word *ming* or *yeh*.

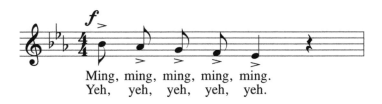

Ming, ming, ming, ming, ming.
Yeh, yeh, yeh, yeh, yeh.

FIGURE 7.7. MING/YEH.

Now return to your singing voice, quickly singing one or more of your practice exercises on the *noo* or *nee* vowel. You should "feel" that your sung sound is now more high and forward than it was before, and certainly in a higher and more forward place than when you speak. In your practice, use the following sequence to create a healthy singing sound.

1. Sigh downward on *oo*.

2. Perform the *ming/yeh exercise* several times at a *forte* dynamic.

3. Sigh downward on *oo* using the "up and over gesture," ending with the heel of your hand on your forehead.

4. Immediately sing through one or more of your practice exercises.

Remember that you create the unique sound of your voice through this balancing of space in your voice (learned from the downward sigh) and the color experienced through the *ming/yeh exercise.*

BODY AWARENESS AS YOU SING ———

Creating and Reinforcing Awareness

In addition to kinesthetic and tactile awareness, singers need full experience of their own emotions and the emotions inspired by the music they're singing. All this inner awareness, together with auditory and visual information, is called inclusive awareness. Inclusive awareness contains all relevant information in the moment the information is needed. Inclusive awareness is a rich and pleasurable state of being, one of the reasons people love singing so much. As a bonus, inclusive awareness and an accurate Body Map are effective proof against problems that plague singers, truly protecting singers over a lifetime. (p. 13)

Profound embodiment is also the key to ensemble. Singers' continuous, intimate, often intense awareness of their own bodies (sensations, movements, and emotions) is the ideal condition for feeling and responding to each other and to the conductor. Then a chorus is a chorus and not just a collection of individuals singing at the same time. The many choral conductors who have helped their singers regain full body awareness as they sing are surprised and delighted by the terrific difference embodiment makes in the quality of the singing. (p. 14)

—Barbara Conable
The Structures and Movement
of Breathing

If one wanted an overall objective for great singing, it would be to create *inclusive awareness* at all times: that is, being aware of your entire body at all times. The reason for this is the fact that, heretofore, musicians have always believed they have only five senses to work with as teachers. The fact is that there are *six* senses, the sixth being *kinesthesia,* narrowly defined as the feeling of the body when engaged in musical performance. For musicians, hearing and kinesthesia must be their most important senses. With every practice session, a reprioritizing of the senses must take place if vocal technique is to be not only learned but also easily recalled.

While it may seem difficult to achieve a type of inclusive awareness that includes kinesthesia, it is actually relatively simple. Being aware is a state that is easily achievable once we understand that the world creates in us a state of unawareness. Unawareness can be countered by simply calling yourself into a state of awareness by asking in varying ways if you are aware of yourself. Simplistic as it sounds, this call to awareness is a powerful force, and is the key to vocal health and development. Body Mapping, aural awareness, listening, and feeling are all components of inclusive awareness.

As you sing, ask yourself:

1. Am I singing with my whole body?

2. Is my body lengthening between points one and four of my core alignment (see Figure 1.1)?

3. Is air coming into my body like a wave from top to bottom?

4. Do I feel energy from my legs moving downward, almost rooting me to the ground?

LESSON NINE

ENERGIZING SOUND
THROUGH PHYSICAL GESTURE

Physical Gestures to Reinforce Good Singing Habits

Throughout *Step by Step* I have made a case for the use of gesture to reinforce proper singing principles. The gestural vocabulary presented here is suggested. Gestures can be combined or modified, and applied to portions or entire exercises, as you deem necessary. Remember that the primary role of these gestures is to ensure that you are employing proper aspects of vocal technique within a group setting. In fact, the use of these gestures will ensure particular elements of vocal technique are being consistently employed and applied. Experiment with adding these gestures to your exercises.

Up and Over

This gesture (Figure 9.1) subconsciously reinforces the concept of making space for sound and maintaining that sound in a high and forward position. It can also suggest a lengthening of the spine and a release of the A/O joint as sound is produced.

FIGURE 9.1. UP AND OVER.

Pointing

Pointing (Figure 9.2) is one of the most useful gestures, and can serve one or many purposes in a practice session. Possible uses of pointing are as follows:

- To clarify the attack of each note.

- To minimize or eliminate the glissando or portamento that causes inaccurate pitch.

- To energize sound.

- To place responsibility for attack and rhythmic exactness upon the singer.

- To infuse a lackluster sound with energy.

- When performed in the right region, to bring more head tone into the sound.

- To provide a tactile symbolization of spiritual commitment brought to the production of sounds.

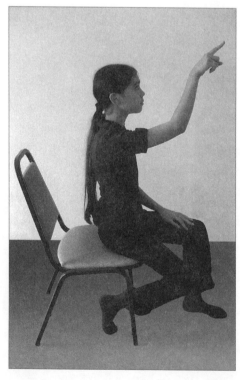

FIGURE 9.2. POINTING GESTURE (NOTE THE CORRECT LOCATION OF THE POINT OF THE FINGER AND ITS DIRECTION).

Heel of Hand on Forehead

One of the most difficult challenges, yet one of the most helpful for improving vocal sound, is to make certain the sound you produce is *always* high and forward. By placing the heel of your hand on your forehead (Figure 9.3), you will subconsciously always place sound in a higher, more forward position.

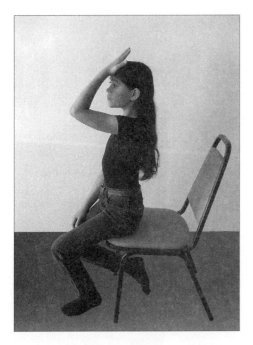 

FIGURE 9.3. HEEL OF HAND ON FOREHEAD.

FIGURE 9.4. FINGER TOSS INTO FOREHEAD.

Finger Toss into Forehead

This gesture (Figure 9.4) is valuable for two reasons. First, it brings head tone into any sound to which it is applied. Second, this is one of the most efficient gestures to take weight out of vocal sound. It is especially valuable for music that requires rhythmic buoyancy in the sound.

Toss Open Leg Lift

This gesture (Figure 9.5) is invaluable for range extension exercises. Lifting your leg while simultaneously opening your arms takes your mind off of the vocal mechanism so the voice can execute the technique required. This gesture is best with exercise melody 4.

FIGURE 9.5. TOSS OPEN LEG LIFT.

FIGURE 9.6. FORWARD SPIN.

Forward Spin

This technique will greatly assist you in learning the concept of the constant and forward movement of air that is crucial to good singing. The gesture (Figure 9.6) not only relays the kinesthetic of forward-moving air, but it also represents the energy that must be contained in that forward movement.

Breath Kneading Gesture

This is one of the most effective gestures for learning the complex act described as support. In one gesture (Figure 9.7) you experience the feeling of on-the-breath singing and supported sound around an alignment core and low center of breath.

FIGURE 9.7. BREATH KNEADING
GESTURE.

FIGURE 9.8. FORWARD BALL TOSS.

Forward Ball Toss

This gesture (Figure 9.8) is most useful when applied to range extension exercises. The throwing gesture reinforces not only the energy required to sing a leap, but it also reinforces the concept of an increase in space for all singing that is in the upper register or that leaps into the upper register.

Dipping

This movement (Figure 9.9) assists range extension exercises, especially Melody 4. The body moves downward as sound ascends, which helps to keep support low in the body.

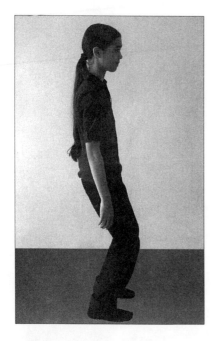
FIGURE 9.9. DIPPING.

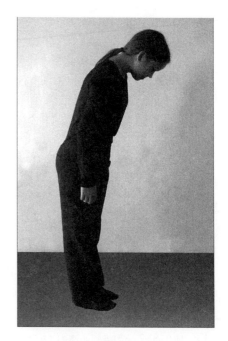
FIGURE 9.10. BODY TIP.

Body Tip

Tipping the head (see Figure 9.10) especially for male voices, helps to maintain space in the upper register and assists in closing the vowel. These two techniques in combination are often referred to as *covering*, which means to achieve a more focused and beautiful tone.

Breath Anchor and Space Umbrella Diagonal

These two gestures (Figure 9.11) should be done concurrently for maximum effect. The left hand formed into a fist symbolizes the exact location or kinesthetic sensation of breath placement within the core of the body. The hand over the head represents the space that is also needed in all well-produced vocal sound. Note that there is a straight but *diagonal* line formed between the left-handed fist and the right-handed umbrella over the back of the head.

FIGURE 9.11. BREATH ANCHOR AND
SPACE UMBRELLA DIAGONAL.

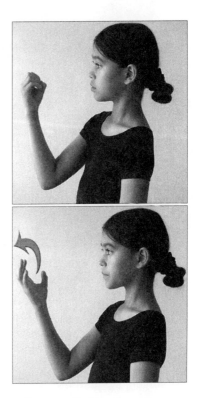

FIGURE 9.12. FLICK AND
LIGHTEN: TIP OF THE
TONGUE *L* FINGER FLICK.

Flick and Lighten (Tip of the Tongue *L* Finger Flick)

This gesture (Figure 9.12) is most valuable when faster, lighter, and more quickly executed consonants are desired. Performed in the area of the forehead, it can also serve to bring more head tone into the sound. The gesture is most effective when teaching Americans how to quickly articulate the tip of the tongue *L*.

Finger Twirl over the Head

This spinning gesture (Figure 9.13) directly over the crown of the head accomplishes several objectives. First, it infuses head tone into the sound. Second, it teaches the choir how to "spin," or allow the sound to be energized in a forward-moving fashion.

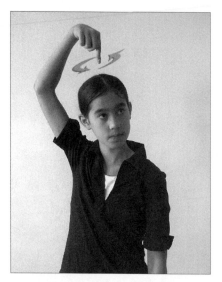

FIGURE 9.13. FINGER TWIRL OVER THE HEAD.

FIGURE 9.14. DROOPING HANDS.

Drooping Hands

As singers descend into their lower register, the sound often becomes "tight" because the vocal mechanism is "held" or possibly begins to rise. This gesture (Figure 9.14) infuses an immediate freedom into all tight and held sounds.

Resonance Swimming Cap Peel

For choral sounds that require maximum output of resonance from the singers, maximum use must be made of *all* resonances possible. An efficient and easy way to maximize your resonance capability is to use the analogy of a person taking a swimming cap slowly off the head and then filling the head area exposed by the removed cap (Figure 9.15). Use this gesture for crescendo and decrescendo.

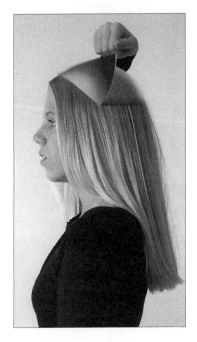

FIGURE 9.16. HIGH AND FORWARD
FINGER WAND (THE *OO* MAGNET).

FIGURE 9.15.
RESONANCE SWIMMING CAP PEEL.

High and Forward Finger Wand (The oo Magnet)

The *oo* vowel is problematic because American singers tend to produce the vowel with too backward a placement (i.e., a "jowel" vowel). By singing the *oo* vowel into the finger held at eye level and forward of the face (Figure 9.16), the vowel is teased into a higher and more forward position.

Tossing Clap

This is a valuable gesture (Figure 9.17) adapted from Dalcroze technique that allows a singer to kinesthetically understand the weight required for any style of music. The key to this gesture is to make certain the clap is thrown from side to side, across the midline of the body. The weight of the clap can be varied to represent the desired stylistic weight to be felt in the sound. The gesture is effective for both adding and taking away weight in all styles of choral music.

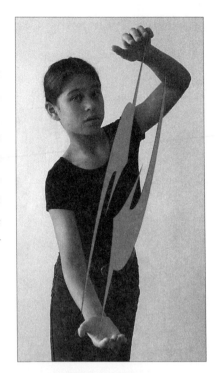

FIGURE 9.17. TOSSING CLAP.

Hand Dab for Energy

It can be difficult to comprehend how to energize a dull sound. Many times, adding a simple hand dab will effect this (Figure 9.18). Any direct, energetic motion that does not lock on the rebound will accomplish this purpose.

FIGURE 9.18. HAND DAB FOR ENERGY.

Hand Smoothing Gesture

The concept of legato, or the maintenance of legato, can be difficult to maintain. Again, the use of a hand gesture (Figures 9.19 and 9.20) coupled with an appropriate vocalise can accomplish this. The gesture should be a smooth and continuous motion from left to right. The hand can be held parallel to the floor, but an inherent danger in this position is that the resulting sound may be overly dark and lack spaciousness. A better hand position is one similar to the action of mixing water and soap together in a bath. The gesture should be done with only one hand.

FIGURE 9.19. HAND SMOOTHING
GESTURE, LEFT TO RIGHT:
BEGINNING POSITION.

FIGURE 9.20. HAND SMOOTHING
GESTURE, LEFT TO RIGHT:
OUTSIDE POSITION.

Congealing Sound Mixing Gesture

At times it may difficult to understand how to mix various aspects of vocal technique into an appropriately healthy and free vocal sound. Marrying the concepts of vertical spaciousness with a high and forward vocal placement is especially difficult. This can be accomplished fairly simply by using the shown in Figures 9.21 through 9.24 gesture.

Begin the gesture as an overhead umbrella, similar to the one employed for space in the sigh. Bring the hands over the head, and then move them together toward a point that forms a 45-degree angle. Stop the forward movement when you hear a good sound—that is, when the sound is clearest and most beautiful. Overextension of the hands will result in a sound that is overly bright. Stopping prematurely will produce a sound that is placed in the rear of the mouth and spread.

FIGURE 9.21. CONGEALING
SOUND MIXING GESTURE:
BEGINNING POSITION.

FIGURE 9.22. CONGEALING
SOUND MIXING GESTURE:
MIDDLE POSITION.

FIGURE 9.23. CONGEALING SOUND MIXING GESTURE: END POSITION.

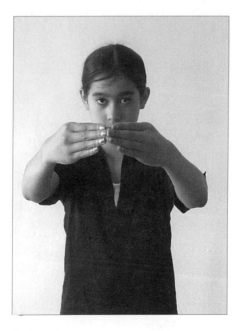

FIGURE 9.24. CONGEALING SOUND MIXING GESTURE:
UNDESIRABLE END POSITION.

Linguine Pull Gesture

Singers often have difficulty singing through vowel sounds and maintaining the forward spin in the sound. In addition, they may have problems maintaining the high and forward placement of vowel sounds. The linguine pull gesture (Figures 9.25 and 9.26) not only accomplishes all those goals, it also ensures a rhythmically vital constant forward movement of the sound(s). Take care to ensure that the gesture is performed in a high and forward fashion.

FIGURE 9.25. LINGUINE PULL GESTURE: FRONT VIEW.

FIGURE 9.26. LINGUINE PULL GESTURE: SIDE VIEW.

Upward Cheekbone Brush

This physical gesture (Figure 9.27) is useful to reinforce high and forward placement. The heel of both hands gently brushes the cheekbones and moves upward at a 45-degree angle.

FIGURE 9.27. UPWARD CHEEKBONE BRUSH.

Toss Open Leg Lift

This gesture (Figure 9.28) is invaluable for range extension exercises. When the leg is lifted and the arms are simultaneously opened, it takes the singer's mind off of the vocal mechanism so the voice can execute the technique required.

FIGURE 9.28. TOSS OPEN LEG LIFT.

Sound Rolling Gesture
(for *piano* and *pianissimo* dynamics)

In addition to closing the vowel and maintaining vertical spaciousness to achieve a vibrant, in-tune *piano* or *pianissimo* sound, it is often helpful to roll the sound forward in the face (Figures 9.29 and 9.30), maintaining a high and forward vowel placement. This will enable you to diminish the *piano* dynamic toward ***pp*** or ***ppp***.

FIGURE 9.29. SOUND ROLLING GESTURE FOR *PIANO* AND *PIANISSIMO* DYNAMICS: BEGINNING POSITION.

FIGURE 9.30. SOUND ROLLING GESTURE FOR *PIANO* AND *PIANISSIMO* DYNAMICS: ENDING POSITION.

Consonant Wisp Gesture

In some situations, it is desirable to have phrases with light endings that seem to disappear (Figures 9.31 and 9.32).

FIGURE 9.31. CONSONANT WISP GESTURE: BEGINNING POSITION.

FIGURE 9.32. CONSONANT WISP GESTURE: ENDING POSITION.

Upward Toss (for sound weight reduction)

Many times, singers will carry too much vocal weight into the choral sound in pieces that require a more transparent texture, such as madrigals and music of the Renaissance. This gesture (Figures 9.33 and 9.34) is especially valuable for pieces that move at a fast tempo, when the consonant weight both causes the pitch to go flat and slows the forward movement of the musical line.

FIGURE 9.33. UPWARD TOSS FOR SOUND WEIGHT REDUCTION:
BEGINNING POSITION.

FIGURE 9.34. UPWARD TOSS FOR SOUND WEIGHT REDUCTION:
ENDING POSITION.

BASICS OF DICTION _____

Basic Diction Pitfalls

There are many books written that clarify the intricacies of sung diction. However, for the purposes of basic voice study, vigilance over several problems will correct the major diction stumbling blocks for most singers.

The Schwa

Of all diction problems, this one is perhaps the most prevalent among singers. By definition, a *schwa* is *an unaccented or unstressed neutral syllable.* In vocal performance, these syllables must be muted. Schwas can take many visual forms, and they can occupy positions within words at the beginning, middle, or end of words. There may also be more than one schwa within a word.

There is also a secondary form of a schwa: a syllable that needs to be muted because of dialect.

The schwa is indicated in the examples below by boldface type.

moth**er** (omit the "r")	Fath**er** (omit the "r")
heav**en**	di**vine**
re**mem**brance	nev**er** (omit the "r")
low**est**	child**ren**
cor**ner**	**o**pen
ap**ple**	lit**tle**

Follow the procedure below for all schwas.

Learning Schwas

1. Identify the syllable in the word that is a schwa.

2. Circle the schwa syllable in red.

3. Wrap your lips around the sound for the syllable containing the schwa.

4. Make sure the lips participate in the muting (de-stressing) of the schwa.

5. Be certain the schwa sound does not become dark in color. Schwa sounds must also be spacious, high, and forward. Always maintain the internal color and integrity of the vowel.

Diphthongs

Diphthongs are syllables composed of two vowel sounds. In solo singing, the instruction for diphthongs is to merely slip the second vowel in before moving to the next vowel sound.

The Troublesome R

The consonant *r* is extremely troublesome for American singers. The problem is that, without instruction, Americans often sing the reflexive American *r.* An *r* sung in this way is extremely damaging to the vowel that follows for two reasons. First, the American *r* usually sends the sound backward in the throat, and second, it tends to twist or distort the vowel sound that immediately follows. To eliminate this problem, never sing an *r* before a consonant and single flip or roll an *r* when it occurs before a vowel.

The Tip of the Tongue L

For American singers, this consonant is problematic because its American pronunciation ensures the placement of the sound in the middle to rear of the mouth. To eliminate this problem, articulate the *l* with the tip of the tongue contacting the area just above the gum line of the upper teeth.

BEING MUSICAL: THE ART OF PHRASING

The Noble *Day-Tay* System of Aural Melodic Organization

I have often witnessed Weston Noble (one of America's premier choral conductors) employing this system of teaching phrasing regardless of his singers' musical background. The *day-tay* system is Noble's attempt to merge the count singing principles espoused by Robert Shaw with the note grouping ideas of James Morgan Thurmond. Only recently did I come to a deep appreciation (and understanding) of the genius of this stupendously simple but elegant system. This system can be used with any singer because it uses only two syllables, regardless of the meter being performed. It is a highly effective method for learning to phrase musically and artistically.

Thurmond marks individual notes of a musical line with either *A* for *accented* or *U* for *unaccented*. While this method visually explains the principles of note grouping, such a labeling system does not easily transfer to musical sound. Noble uses a system that uses only two sounds—*day* and *tay*—that substitute for Thurmond's *U* and *A* that can be construed as theoretical without basis in sound. Simply stated, Noble's system asks singers to place a *day* syllable on each note that should receive musical weight (or stress) and a *tay* syllable on each unstressed note of the musical phrase. Decisions regarding placement of *day* syllables require personal musical judgment. For example, consider the opening phrase of *For Unto Us a Child Is Born* from Handel's *Messiah* (Figure 11.1):

---

x = space or daylight between notes

For	un-to	us		a	child	is	born;		un-to		us,
Tay	*day-tay*	*tay*	*x*	*tay*	*tay*	*tay*	*day-tay*	*x*	*tay tay*	*x*	*day—*

For	un-to	us	a	child	is		born;		un-to	us,
Tay	*x day-tay*	*tay*	*tay*	*tay*	*tay*	*x*	*day-tay*	*x*	*tay day*	*day—*

FIGURE 11.1.

Both phrasing choices are possible, and there are many more combinations. But what lies at the foundation of note grouping principles is that musical phrasing is about choices.

Nouns and Verbs; Adjectives and Adverbs

> The presence of a text gives singers a decided advantage in realizing the rules in our poem. Since articles and adjectives (usually weaker words) naturally lead to nouns, pronouns, and verbs (usually stronger words), a well-set text enhances the "weak to strong" principle. (p. 87)

> —Weston Noble
> in *Creating the Special World*

There are built-in suggestions for singers with regard to phrasing. In general, nouns and verbs occur on beats that should be stressed or weighted, and adjectives and adverbs generally occupy beats that should receive less stress or weight. An analysis of the placement of these parts of speech provides germinal ideas about the musical phrase. It is then up to you to apply *day-tay* syllables that reflect the structure of the text. From the very beginning of the learning process for any piece of music, the weights and unstressed syllables of the musical line must be integral to the musicing. *Day-tay* syllables provide a simple yet organic way of learning musical phrasing in union with the elements of pitch and rhythm. These syllables also provide for an almost infinite way to learn the many variations of musical phrasing known as *interpretation*.

Your assignment of *day* and *tay* is directly related to *your* ideas of how notes are grouped within a musical phrase. There are many options you could pursue, given the rhythmic values within each phrase. The left column in Figure 11.4 represents what Noble refers to as *square phrasing*. In the right column are the new note grouping possibilities. After you determine exactly what type of phrasing you desire, then you can assign *day* to the note immediately under the beginning of a bracket and *tay* to the notes that follow.

Now experiment with placing *day* and *tay* in different places in the exercise melodies to achieve different phrasings. Here are four possibilities:

A.

tay   tay   day   tay   tay   day   day   tay   tay   day   tay

B.

tay   tay   tay   tay   tay   tay   day   tay   tya   tay   day

FIGURE 11.2. EXERCISE MELODY 3 WITH TWO *DAY-TAY* VARIATIONS.

A.

tay   tay   tay   tay   tay   tay

tay   day   tay   day   tay —   tay   tay   tay

B.

tay   tay   day   tay   tay   day

tay   tay   tay   tay   tay —   day   tay   tay

FIGURE 11.3. EXERCISE MELODY 6 WITH TWO *DAY-TAY* VARIATIONS.

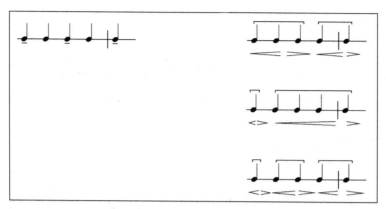

FIGURE 11.4. EXAMPLE OF NOTE GROUPING.

Noble's Phrasing Guidelines

In his book, *Creating the Special World* (GIA, G-6529), Weston Noble writes that there are five rules that apply specifically to Baroque phrasing, but they can be generalized to all subsequent periods. To these five rules, I have added a sixth (below). The *day-tay* syllables can be applied with these rules in mind. Noble's descriptions of each category are both concise and wonderful. Study pages 78–90 in his book for detailed explanations of his rules.

RULE 1   WEAK TO STRONG

RULE 2   SHORT TO LONG

RULE 3   REPEATED NOTES

RULE 4   CHANGE OF SONG

RULE 5   JUST BECAUSE I FEEL LIKE IT

RULE 6   ENERGIZE ALL RESTS

Noble uses a short poem to summarize all of the above rules and to help him arrive at phrasing decisions:

WEAK TO STRONG, SHORT TO LONG
REPEATED NOTES, CHANGE OF SONG.

Directors do not have time to explain every moment when Baroque phrasing is desired. It can be beyond the comprehension of the singers as well. If the instructor sings a desired passage with the desired result of this type of phrasing but substitutes a "day" for every *thetic* moment and a "tay" for every *arsic* moment, the choir will sing back what was emulated, and it will follow every basic rule of Baroque phrasing. And the music will immediately dance! The choir will respond with relative ease, simply because it feels so natural to be sung this way! (p. 86)

Shaw gave us a new definition of rhythm. Rhythm is obviously timing, but now we must add the word SPACING! There is a world of difference! (p. 87)

>   —Weston Noble
>   in *Creating the Special World*

ABOUT THE AUTHOR _____

James Jordan is considered to be one of the most influential choral conductors and educators in America. His over thirty publications, including books covering rehearsal and teaching pedagogy, conducting technique, and the spirituality of musicing, as well as numerous DVDs and recordings, have brought about far-reaching pedagogical and philosophical changes not only in choral music but also in the worlds of orchestral conducting, wind conducting, piano, and music education. *The Choral Journal* has described his writings as "visionary." Renowned composer Morten Lauridsen dedicated the third movement of his *Midwinter Songs* to him.

One of the country's leading choral artists, Dr. Jordan is Professor and Senior Conductor at Westminster Choir College of Rider University, where he conducts the Westminster Williamson Voices and the Westminster Schola Cantorum, and teaches undergraduate and graduate choral conducting. Over thirty works have been premiered by the Westminster Williamson Voices, including the works of Mantyjaarvi, Custer, Ames, Hill, Whitbourn, Henson, and Wilberg. Dr. Jordan also conducts Anam Cara (www.anamcarachoir.com), a professional choral ensemble based in Philadelphia, that has also received critical acclaim for its recordings. The *American Record Review* wrote that Anam Cara "is a choir to please the fussiest choral connoisseur" and called their inaugural recording, *Innisfree*, "skillful and shining," "glowing," "supremely accomplished" with a "tone that produces a wide range of effects from vocal transparency to rich, full-throated glory."

Dr. Jordan is one of the country's most prolific writers on the subjects of the philosophy of music making and choral teaching. His trilogy of books on the philosophy and spirituality of musicing—*The Musician's Soul, The Musician's Spirit,* and *The Musician's Walk*—have made a deep and profound impact upon musicians and teachers around the world.

Dr. Jordan is also Executive Editor of the *Evoking Sound Choral Series* (GIA), which now includes over one hundred published works. In addition, he delivers over thirty workshops and keynote addresses each year in addition to an extensive conducting schedule.

Dr. Jordan has had the unique privilege of studying with several of the landmark teachers of the twentieth century. He was a student of Elaine Brown, Wilhelm Ehmann, and Frauke Haasemann. He completed his Ph.D. in Psychology of Music under Edwin Gordon. He has been the recipient of many awards for his contributions to the profession.

Dr. Jordan's lecture/teaching schedule and writings are detailed on his Web site (www.evokingsound.com) and his publisher's Web site (www.giamusic.com/jordan).